# A Dozen Dramatic Walks

*in*

# Devon

## James Clancy

*and*

## Simone Stanbrook-Byrne

CULM VALLEY PUBLISHING

Published by

Culm Valley Publishing Ltd
Culmcott House
Mill Street, Uffculme
Cullompton, Devon
EX15 3AT, UK
Tel: +44(0)1884 849085
Fax: +44(0)1884 840251
E-mail: info@culmvalleypublishing.co.uk
Website: www.culmvalleypublishing.co.uk

While every effort has been made to ensure the accuracy of the information contained in
this book, the publisher and authors accepts no liability for incorrect information
regarding public footpaths and rights of way. Neither Culm Valley Publishing Ltd nor
the authors shall be liable for any damages whatsoever arising in any way from the use of
or inability to use this book, or any material contained within it, or from any action or
decision taken as a result of using this book. Follow the country code.

First published 2011

ISBN 978-1-907942-00-6 paperback

British Library Cataloguing-in-Publication Data
A catalogue record for this book is available from the British Library

Typeset by Culm Valley Publishing Ltd
Printed and bound by T.J. International Ltd, Padstow, Cornwall
Cover image: Starehole Cove, Salcombe

# Contents

# Introduction

Writing this walking guide has been great fun. The authors have enjoyed all the drama very much – the effort of getting to the highest points, the route-finding when paths disappeared, the slogging through storms, the fabulous views and the reward of ending the day where we planned to be.

By virtue of their nature 'dramatic walks' can involve challenging terrain so whenever you embark on a walk common sense must prevail: be properly shod and take care where you put your feet, be prepared for any kind of weather, take food and first aid supplies with you and make sure someone knows where you're going. Mobile phones are often useless in the middle of nowhere.

We also feel it's **imperative** that you take the **correct OS map** with you plus a **compass**, and are conversant with their use. Our sketch maps are precisely that – sketches – and are for rough guidance only and are not to scale.

You know you've had a good day's walking when you get home safely at the end of it and haven't been overtaken by the drama.

**Useful websites:**
The army train regularly on parts of Dartmoor so do ensure you check the following website before setting out: www.dartmoor-ranges.co.uk/index.html Alternatively the firing programme is available on: 0800 458 4868. Another useful site which gives tips for moorland treks is: www.tourbytor.co.uk/equip_walk.php

**Follow the countryside code:**
www.naturalengland.org.uk/ourwork/enjoying/countrysidecode/def ault.aspx

# Disciaimer

**Points that should be borne in mind on any route – dramatic or not:**

Public footpaths can be legally re-routed from the path shown on the map. In such cases they are usually clearly signposted. Where this has happened before the time of writing it has been noted in the text.

Most public footpaths are on private land. Please respect this.

Don't be surprised to find livestock grazing on public footpaths – and treat all animals with caution and respect.

If a field is planted with crops across a footpath, provision is usually made around the edge of the field.

Landmarks can change: trees and hedges may disappear; streams can dry up in warm weather; stiles turn into gates and vice versa; fences appear where previously there was no boundary. Even views are different as the seasons change. In such cases a modicum of common sense must be exercised – in conjunction with the map.

Public footpaths are at times blocked by barbed wire etc. Should this render the route impassable find the shortest detour around that section.

Please leave gates as you find them and if you have to climb them do so at the hinge end where it's stronger.

Exercise caution on wet stiles – they can be extremely slippery.

Take all your rubbish with you, don't damage anything during the walk and don't pick plants.

Keep your dogs under proper control.

We hope that you enjoy these walks without mishap, but urge you to exercise common sense at all times! Neither the authors nor Culm Valley Publishing Ltd. accepts responsibility for any misadventure which may occur during or arise from these walks and suggested routes.

6

## Acknowledgements

Many people have pitched in and helped during the production of this book but particular thanks must go to:

Brian and Jenny Willan for support, advice and a fabulous office;

to Sandy Smith for geological pointers;

to the troupes of friends who let us drag them round some of the tougher routes (we'd like to say without complaint but that wouldn't be true, would it, Yvette?);

to Tony, Nic, Ella and William for support and sustenance.

The Valley of Rocks

# Walk Locations

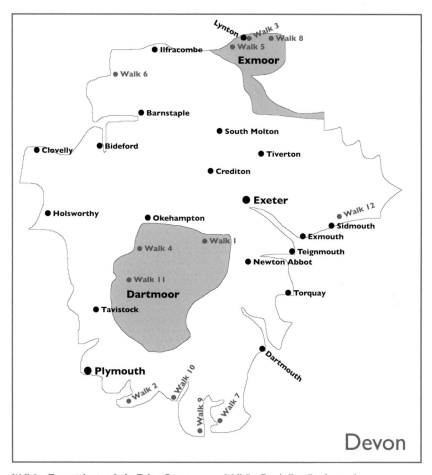

| Walk 1 | Drewsteignton & the Teign Gorge | Walk 7 | Exotic East Portlemouth |
|---|---|---|---|
| Walk 2 | Noss Mayo & the Warren | Walk 8 | The Doone Valley |
| Walk 3 | Little Switzerland | Walk 9 | Bolt Head & Soar Mill Cove |
| Walk 4 | Meldon & the High Tors | Walk 10 | Bigbury-on-Sea & Burgh Island |
| Walk 5 | Trentishoe & the Heddon Valley | Walk 11 | Tavy Cleave |
| Walk 6 | North Devon's Glorious Beaches | Walk 12 | Branscombe & the Hooken Undercliff |

## Walk 1
## Drewsteignton & the Teign Gorge


*The starting point is in the idyllic village of Drewsteignton. The route offers thirst-quenching, high views and tranquil valley walking. Between the two are some steep paths to negotiate so strong shoes are, as always, very important.*

---

**Map:** OS Outdoor Leisure 28, Dartmoor 1:25 000
**Start point:** Drewsteignton Village. Grid ref SX735908
**Distance:** 6 miles / 10km (6.5 miles / 10.5km if easier option taken when descending to Teign Valley)
**Parking:** In Village Square or in designated parking area which is signed from The Square and is more easily accessed than it may at first appear
**Refreshments:** The Drewe Arms, Drewsteignton, a delightful, very traditional pub: 01647 281224; The Fingle Bridge Inn (also known as The Angler's Rest) with a lovely riverside setting: 01647 281287
**Toilets:** Public toilets can be found clearly signposted in the village of Drewsteignton and at Fingle Bridge
**Nearby places to stay:** The Old Inn, Drewsteignton: 01647 281276
**Nearby places of interest:** Castle Drogo (NT): 01647 433306
**Possible birds include:** Chaffinch, chiffchaff, dipper, great spotted woodpecker, grey wagtail, magpie, pied wagtail, raven, song thrush, swift, willow warbler, wren
**Authors' tip:** The 15th C. Church of the Holy Trinity and its pretty churchyard are surrounded by some very picturesque thatched cottages. Allow time to explore and do it justice

---

Turn left out of The Square, following the road as it then bends right signed for Castle Drogo (you'll see the sign here pointing left for public toilets). About 150 metres further take a footpath left off the road. This goes downhill and bends to the right. At a fingerpost keep ahead on the footpath signed for Castle Drogo and its shop and café, ignoring the bridleway to the left. The stem of this post also indicates the Two Moors Way, an 'M' above a 'W'.

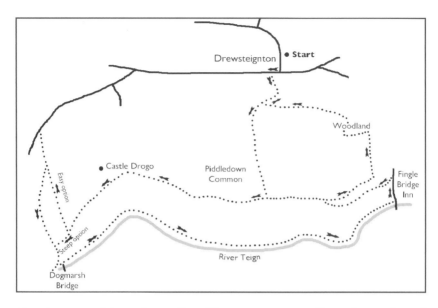

Continue up this path, scaling 50 steps to a gate. Pass through and continue, you soon emerge from the woodland path through another gate and into a field. Keep ahead up the field with the fence on your right. Pause at the metal farm gate to enjoy views back to Drewsteignton and the beautiful countryside beyond. Find the stile to the right of the farm gate and cross it, glancing at the inscription '1976' which someone has carved here to remind us of droughts and hot summer days. Pass through the gorse and continue through the field with the fence and gorse to your right.

Continue to the right hand corner of the field to the kissing gate under the trees. The land you are crossing now is Piddledown Common and you may well see ponies grazing in this area. Go ahead to the fingerpost and turn right along The Hunter's Path. Admire the stunning views as you walk above the Teign Gorge. To your right you will soon have your first glimpse of Castle Drogo, England's youngest castle, now belonging to The National Trust, and you may hear the river below in the gorge. Along this path from time to time you will encounter little paths to the left leading to view

*Along the River Teign at Dogmarsh Bridge*

points. They are worth checking out but are precipitous so take care on the edges.

Continue ahead at the next two fingerposts marked Hunter's Path and Dogmarsh Bridge, the view opens up now to the castle, the Teign Gorge and the tors of Dartmoor beyond. From the path below the area of the castle glance back – the gorge is good in that direction too.

As the path enters trees and takes a definite right turn (1¼ miles from first joining the Hunter's Path) you have an option. For those not wishing to negotiate the steep descent into the valley, go right with the path. Eventually you reach two gates in quick succession and then meet a tarmac drive. Turn left, signposted to the Fisherman's Path, to rejoin the main route at (*) below. The more intrepid can keep straight ahead on a path through the trees. Good luck! Follow this stony path between rocks and follow it downhill (a short incline off the downhill path leads to another rocky viewpoint which can be enjoyed if you so desire). Your descending path leads steeply downhill to the right, keep your knees in low gear. Eventually it becomes a softer path underfoot, although still steep, and passes through woodland. At the bottom turn left, (*) this is where the earlier detour rejoins. The path is still going downhill but now less steeply.

At the bottom you reach the river and turn left, signposted Fingle Bridge, Fisherman's Path (this stretch is shown on the map as The Dartmoor Way.) There is an attractive suspension footbridge here which gives good views along the river, but don't cross over. Continue along the valley path, keeping the river on your right and passing an impressive weir. This is a lovely, tranquil path with occasional sets of steps. Keep going. When the path forks keep beside the river, although the two options do merge again. At Fingle Bridge seize the opportunity to watch birds on the river while consuming cream teas or ale as your fancy takes you.

### Castle Drogo

This magnificent building above the Teign Gorge is a relatively modern monument to a long-gone romantic age. Commissioned by business tycoon Julius Drewe during the early part of the 20th Century, the Lutyens-designed Castle Drogo is England's youngest castle and, despite its present size, is much scaled back from the original grandiose plans. Completion of the building took a couple of decades, although it was habitable for a few years prior to being fully finished in 1930. Julius Drewe died in 1931 at which point the castle passed to his son, Basil. In 1974 Basil's descendants gave the property to The National Trust – at the time it was the most modern building in Trust ownership. The castle houses family collections and furnishings, many of which pre-date the building. Interestingly, electricity derived from water-power was installed from the outset – quite an innovation at the time but necessary to power the lift which helped the by-then disabled Julius Drewe to get around his home.

Leaving the Inn, walk along the lane away from the bridge for a couple of hundred metres then turn left uphill on a wooded footpath signed to the Hunter's Path, Castle Drogo and Drewsteignton (indirectly). This is a steep incline but you are rewarded with wonderful views of the gorge. Keep ascending and don't give up at this stage; landing the air ambulance would be tricky. At a T-junction turn right on the Hunter's Path signposted for Drewsteignton. This is a pleasant woodland path with an occasional inviting bench and, at one point, a particularly magnificent beech tree which may be worth hugging if you're having a six-arm moment.

When you reach a crossing forestry track go straight over, signposted simply as 'path'. Continue on this track ignoring any right or left turns until you meet a T-junction at which a finger post indicates that you have just come along the Hunter's Path. Turn right here heading slightly downhill. Reach another fingerpost and go straight ahead for Drewsteignton. At the next sign go right, still heading for Drewsteignton. You will recognise this junction from earlier in the walk and from here retrace your steps along the short final stretch back to your car.

*Hunter's Path*    © *Simone Stanbrook-Byrne*    **The Teign Gorge**    © *Simone Stanbrook-Byrne*

*Walk 2*
# Noss Mayo & The Warren

*This lovely walk takes in the drama of South Devon's coastline together with some idyllic creeks and a beautiful village with excellent hostelries. The walking is relatively easy although there are descents to the beaches if you decide to visit them – which we would strongly recommend.*

| | |
|---|---|
| **Map:** OS Outdoor Leisure 20, South Devon 1:25 000 | |
| **Start point:** Noss Mayo. Grid ref SX547474 | |
| **Distance:** 5 miles / 8km | |
| **Parking:** Car park in Noss Mayo next to tennis courts | |
| **Refreshments:** The Ship Inn, Noss Mayo: 01752 872387; The Swan Inn, Noss Mayo: 01752 872392 | |
| **Toilets:** None en route other than in the Inns | |
| **Possible birds include:** Blackbird, blue tit, buzzard, carrion crow, chaffinch, cormorant, little egret, goldfinch, greenfinch, gulls of various hues, house martin, house sparrow, jackdaw, kestrel, long-tailed tit, magpie, mallard, pied wagtail, raven, robin, shag, sparrow hawk, stonechat, swallow, wheatear, whitethroat, woodpigeon, wren | |
| **Nearby places to stay:** Revelstoke Coombe, Noss Mayo: 01752 872663; Worswell Barton Farmhouse B&B, Noss Mayo: 01752 872977 | |
| **Nearby places of interest:** Saltram (NT), Plympton: 01752 333503 | |
| **Authors' tip:** After the walk why not drive to Wembury with its NT Tea Shop right on the beach? | |

Leave the car park and turn left along the lane, passing a playground and a gate on the left into the Woodland Trust-owned Brooking's Down Wood. Don't enter the woods but continue along the lane past houses until you leave the majority of buildings behind and reach a pair of semi-detached houses with barns on your right. Continue past them heading uphill along the track.

This track meets a lane, turn left for about 40 metres and then take the footpath on the right over a stile. You are entering the NT area of The Warren where there is another car park. This path is a link to the South West Coast Path. It passes through a gate, beyond which you go right to join the main coast path, the sea is down to

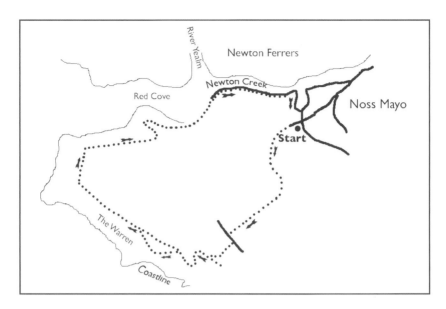

your left and Wembury Bay ahead with Great Mew Stone loafing around offshore.

Soon you approach Warren Cottage. Just before you reach it it's worth taking the left fork down off the main coast path, as this is an open, airy path and will lead you to lovely Warren Beach. If you prefer an easier route you can stay on the main track which will eventually be re-joined by this lower path. On a clear day you can see the Eddystone Lighthouse out to sea, 13 miles SW of Plymouth.

Keep a lookout for a post which indicates that you're at the point of access to Warren Beach (should you miss this post and end up a little further on at a fence with a stile you've gone too far – go back and find the post!). The beach is worth visiting via the steps you will see leading down the cliff, there are some good, flat rocks on which to picnic and nice rock pools. Return to the post and, from the direction of your original approach, turn right and start to head uphill (at the time of writing this was the less-trodden of

*Perfect picnic spot at Warren Beach*

the paths). You will quickly go over another crossing path but keep heading uphill from Warren Beach. The path leads uphill to rejoin the main coast path along which you continue as before, the sea still to your left.

As you round the headland Wembury Church comes into view across the bay. Keep on the path as it heads inland along the estuary, the body of water to your left and ahead is called Red Cove. The path continues through Brakehill Plantation and heads inland for a while before returning towards the coast to eventually lead past Battery Cottage on your right. At Battery Cottage look out for the footpath on the left which will take you down to Cellar Beach should you wish to go there. Otherwise continue on the main path past the cottage as it goes through Passage Wood. As the lane widens you will see an information board about this woodland. From here take the lower path going left off the lane, as although it winds back up to the main path you're closer to the water and it's a very idyllic route.

The path goes through a kissing gate beside Ferryman's Cottage and then past an old Toll House which displays the historic tolls payable. Should you slip into a time warp at this point it will cost you 3d to get your pony or ass across the water.

Beyond here continue on the lane as it leads you along the banks of Yealm Pool down to your left and then Newton Creek. About 200 metres from the toll you will see a path down to Kilpatrick Steps. Keep on the main lane, unless you wish to explore, passing the seasonal ferry and enjoying the scenery of the creek. The lane leads past The Ship Inn, which calls loudly, and soon you see the Village Hall ahead. Here bear left with the lane to cross the head of the creek, then continue uphill and back to the area of the village in which you should find your car.

### Eddystone Lighthouse

If you are doing this walk on a clear day the 49 metres high Eddystone Lighthouse can be seen way out to sea. The building which stands today is the fourth to be constructed. The first was a wooden structure designed by Henry Winstanley which was completed in 1698. Five years later, in November 1703, its designer was in residence undertaking some work on the structure when a massive storm blew up. The lighthouse was wiped out and poor old Winstanley went with it. His body was never found. Rudyard's Lighthouse then followed and was first lit in 1709. The third lighthouse to be built on the site is nowadays well-known to the people of Plymouth as its top section, known as Smeaton's tower, was re-erected on Plymouth Hoe. The current lighthouse was built by James Douglass. It was first lit in 1882 and automated in 1982. It is operated by Trinity House, the General Lighthouse Authority, which itself was granted a charter in 1514 by Henry VIII.

*Wembury Bay*

*Walk 3*
# Little Switzerland

*This beautiful route, through an area dubbed Little Switzerland, encompasses stunning river gorges, an iron age hillfort, spectacular coastal scenery and the curious natural phenomena to be found in the Valley of Rocks. There are some steepish ascents and good footwear is essential especially after wet weather.*

---

**Map:** OS Outdoor Leisure 9, Exmoor 1:25 000

**Start point:** Lynmouth. Grid ref SS719498

**Distance:** 5 miles (8km) / 7.5 miles (12km) / 8.25 miles (13.3km) to Lee Abbey plus any exploration of the area

**Parking:** Lynmouth offers numerous places to park. We suggest the Esplanade Car Park with its spectacular view, where, for a reasonably modest sum, you can park all day

**Refreshments:** Lynmouth and Lynton both offer a great choice of restaurants, pubs, cafés, and snack bars. Watersmeet Tea Gardens (NT) are a must (opening times can vary out of season, it's worth checking before you go): 01598 753348. Mother Meldrum's in the Valley of Rocks shouldn't be missed either: 01598 753667. Hewitt's is good for cream teas on the way back: 01598 752293

**Toilets:** These are well-signposted in both towns and are also to be found at Watersmeet and as you enter the Valley of Rocks

**Nearby places to stay:** Blue Ball Inn, Countisbury: 01598 741263 (very dog friendly); Chough's Nest Hotel, Lynton: 01598 753315; Lynton Cottage Hotel, Lynton: 01598 752342; Rock House Hotel, Lynmouth: 01598 753508; Shelley's Hotel, Lynmouth: 01598 753219. Sunny Lyn Holiday Park – camping/caravanning in lovely location by the West Lyn River: 01598 753384

**Nearby places of interest:** Exmoor Coast Boat Trips: 01598 753207. Glen Lyn Gorge, Lynmouth: 01598 753207. Lyn Model Railway, Watersmeet Road, Lynmouth: 01598 753330. Lynmouth Flood Memorial Hall (next to harbour)

**Possible birds include:** Buzzard, dipper, grey wagtail, guillemot, heron, jackdaw, linnet, oystercatcher, pied wagtail, raven, razorbill, rook, song thrush, stonechat, willow warbler

**Authors' tip:** Although not on the route, The Blue Ball Inn at Countisbury is a wonderful, dog-friendly pub for refreshments. From their car park you can walk up through the churchyard and onto the coast path to find exceptional coastal views down towards Lynmouth and beyond

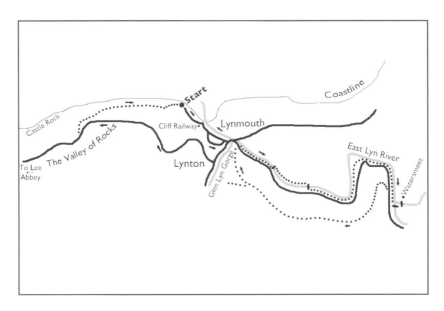

Leave The Esplanade car park and head along the road into Lynmouth. Ahead of you, across the bay, you can see Foreland Point and Countisbury Hill with its transmission mast. Pass the funicular Cliff Railway on your right, unique in that it is the only one in the world powered entirely by water. Bear right with the road as it goes past The Rising Sun XIV century Inn and shortly after this The Bath Hotel, entering the rather quaint shopping precinct. Emerge from here and proceed along Riverside Road to a T-junction. Cross the road (with caution) and descend steps to walk along a stone-walled path beside a car park. The East Lyn River is on your left. Keep along this path. On the far bank of the river you can see Glenville House, Lorna Doone Hotel and some attractive stone cottages. Don't cross the river here but as you continue do spare a glance back towards Lynmouth as the view behind is as picturesque as the one in front.

Soon you reach Middleham Memorial Gardens, the site of the cottages destroyed in the 1952 flood. Visit these via the flight of steps at the far end.

*Waterfall near Watersmeet*

Leave Middleham and continue in the same direction along the river. Cross at the next bridge, signposted for Watersmeet and continue with the river to your right. This is one of our favourite stretches, it becomes very dramatic after heavy rain. After several hundred metres the path ascends. Go with it, admiring views of the river in the gorge below, until you reach a right fork signposted 'Watersmeet Riverside Walk'. Take this and head back down, crossing another bridge and continuing with the river on your left. Keep on this path, passing without crossing another bridge, after which you will see a small stone construction in the wall on your right. A few metres beyond this look out for the Lynrock Ginger Beer bottle set into the wall. This area was the site of a mineral water factory which was another victim of the 1952 flood. Ascend a flight of steps and continue.

Soon you pass the fenced garden of Myrtleberry. Its drive joins from the right but keep ahead on the footpath with the fence on your left. Soon the river opens up slightly, keep ahead as another drive joins from the right. It's worth noticing the amazing plant habitats in the gorge walls through which you are passing. There is an area here for picnics and options on paths, but they all merge in a few metres to continue with the river to your left. Don't be tempted to cross the next bridge, other than to admire the view from the middle, but keep on with the river to your left. Soon you see the welcome sight of Watersmeet House with its tea gardens ahead of you. As the path forks follow the rustic post fence down to the left, crossing first Hoaroak Water and then the East Lyn River – the two waters which meet here. Refresh yourself with tea before continuing.

Leave the tea gardens, re-crossing the two bridges and bearing right after the second bridge. Zigzag up the path leaving the gorge and your route into Watersmeet behind you. At the third bend is a sign 'Lynbridge via The Cleaves'. Follow this up to the lane, it emerges at the staff parking area. Cross the road and pick up the path opposite signposted 'Lynton and Lynmouth via The Cleaves', following this up through the trees. This will lead you to Myrtleberry North, Iron Age Enclosure. Walk across this hillfort to the steps which you can see leading up the hillside ahead of you. Yep, 'fraid so: these are calling you to climb them. There are glorious views as you approach the steps, look right to see Lynton nestling in the surrounding hills.

At the top of the steps keep ahead until the path is joined from the left by the Two Moors Way (denoted by M above W). Bear right here, towards Lynton and Lynmouth, along a lovely stretch of path. There is a steep wooded hanger to your right, rising hillside to your left and eventually the view opens up to the bay with, on a clear day, Wales in the distance across the Bristol Channel. From here you can look down to Lynmouth and your starting point.
The path passes through two footpath gates, still signposted for Lynton and Lynmouth. Look across to the opposite hillside, you will have a good view of Countisbury Hill and The Blue Ball Inn – an excellent hostelry for another time. This path eventually winds downwards to reach a small stony footbridge, then continues up again affording glorious sea views to help you on your way as you climb. Once you're high enough look back along the deeply wooded gorge which you walked through earlier, with farmland rising above it. The view makes the climb very worthwhile.

Eventually you reach a three-fingered footpath sign, at which point head right downhill on the grassy path towards Lynmouth. This is still the Two Moors Way and zigzags all the way back down to Lynmouth, dropping steadily through woodland. Keep downhill with this main path, ignoring any side turns. Nearing Lynmouth you reach a sign welcoming you to the northern end of the Two Moors Way, continue down into the town, passing some attractive cottages before you reach the road. When you reach the road turn left along the pavement, passing Shelley's Hotel on your left. This is Watersmeet Road. Keep left along the road to admire the view along the Glen Lyn Gorge from the bridge. Now cross the road on the bridge and go down a tarmac path between stone walls. Down here on the left you will see a plaque noting the flood height on 15 August 1952 (see feature below).

Retrace your steps through Lynmouth to the Cliff Railway. Those not wishing to take this have the option of using the footpath to ascend to Lynton. This starts just a few metres before the entrance

### The Lynmouth Flood of 1952

Extremes of weather and climate change are frequent features of 21st Century news, but the picturesque village of Lynmouth was devastated by one such phenomenon some decades ago. In August 1952, after 9" (23cm) of rain in 24 hours, the already swollen rivers of the East and West Lyn were unable to cope with the deluge. Lynmouth and its environs bore the full force of millions of tonnes of water and its accompanying debris, resulting in the collapse of 39 buildings and

*Flood marker – Lynmouth*

the deaths of 34 people. Much speculation remains as to the cause of such excessive rainfall. Nowadays a tranquil garden marks the site of destroyed houses but it's sobering to consider the forces of nature which have shaped this landscape over the centuries.

*Looking west along coast from The Valley of Rocks*

to the railway, and is a very steep climb. For those taking the railway, there is a small fare for humans and dogs but the experience is well worth it. Savour it.

Emerging from the railway in Lynton walk ahead on the tarmac road to the main shopping street through the town. This is Lee Road, turn right when you join it, soon passing the Town Hall and later a rather arresting graveyard flanked by some amazing cedar trees. You are heading towards the Valley of Rocks.

Less than a mile from Lynton the road leads into the valley which abounds with semi-wild goats and Exmoor ponies – all part of the natural management of this spectacular area. On your right you will see what is probably one of the most scenic cricket pitches in England. Unless there is something to watch (in which case the walk may take several æons to finish) keep straight on. Ahead of you is the towering mass of Castle Rock. Just after the cricket pitch is Mother Meldrum's Tea Rooms and Gardens. This is another must.

When you feel able to extract yourself from Mother Meldrum's continue along the road towards Castle Rock. Here you have an option.

Those wishing to extend the walk through the valley can do so by following the road across the small roundabout and continuing. This will soon lead you past the fingerpost pointing right to draw your attention to The White Lady. Admire her, then continue if you wish to Lee Abbey, a church retreat and holiday centre. This is about ¾ mile beyond Castle Rock. When you have explored as far as you wish, return to Castle Rock, which the energetic can climb to discover some stunning views. Mother Meldrum's Cave is another point of interest, signposted up the hill on the opposite side of the road.

When you've had your fill of this area, return to Castle Rock and pick up the tarmac coast path, pass the telescope and follow the path back along the cliffs, heading east towards Lynton & Lynmouth. Pause here and glance behind you westwards for one of the most dramatic views in Devon. Continue east on the path as it winds its way back. This is a glorious stretch of coastline, abundant with wild flowers, seabirds, roaming goats and possibly seals. You are being watched by the lighthouse in the distance ahead of you on Foreland Point. This was established in 1900 but automated in 1994. The original keeper's cottage can now be rented for holidays from The National Trust.

Eventually you reach a tree-covered stretch and pass through a gate. Just after the gate leave the main path and go left down a stony path through the trees. This is signed 'Lynmouth ½ mile'. Follow this as it zigzags down. This can be quite rough underfoot.

Part way down this path you will come upon an enticing sign on a gate inviting you to partake of a legendary cream tea at Hewitt's. This is open 12–5 daily, but best to check if visiting out of season. This path descends right into the Esplanade car park from whence you started.

*Walk 4*
# Meldon & the High Tors

*This is one of our very favourite routes taking in the tranquil Meldon Reservoir and a picturesque river valley before venturing up the highest tors of Dartmoor. These include High Willhays, which at 621 metres is the highest point in Great Britain south of the Brecon Beacons.*

| | |
|---|---|
| **Map:** OS Outdoor Leisure 28, Dartmoor 1:25 000 | |
| **Start point:** Meldon Reservoir Car Park. Grid ref SX563917 | |
| **Distance:** 6.5 miles / 10.5km (4.75 miles / 7.6km if easier option taken from Black Tor) | |
| **Parking:** In Meldon Reservoir Car Park as above. | |
| **Refreshments:** None en route. We would recommend The Bearslake Inn at Lake, near Sourton on the A386 to Tavistock: 01837 861334 | |
| **Toilets:** Public toilets can be found in Meldon Reservoir Car Park | |
| **Nearby places to stay:** The Bearslake Inn, Sourton: 01837 861334; Bundu Campsite, Sourton Down: 01837 861611 | |
| **Nearby places of interest:** Okehampton Castle (English Heritage): 01837 52844 | |
| **Possible birds include:** Blue tit, buzzard, chaffinch, coal tit, goldfinch, great tit, grey wagtail, kestrel, magpie, raven, rook, skylark, stonechat, wheatear, willow warbler, woodpigeon, wren | |
| **Authors' tip:** Your journey to the start point may well take you past The Highwayman Inn at Sourton which is worth calling into for its quirky, gothic style. It has been described as the most unusual pub in Britain | |

*Important information*

*Beware, visibility can change rapidly in this area. The walk should not be attempted without a compass and map and the ability to use both! Additionally the army train regularly in this area (Okehampton Range) so do ensure you check the following website before setting out: http://www.dartmoor-ranges.co.uk/index.html Alternatively the firing programme is available on: 0800 458 4868. During the walk you will see subtle evidence of army occupation. Another useful site which gives tips for moorland treks is: http://www.tourbytor.co.uk/equip_walk.php*

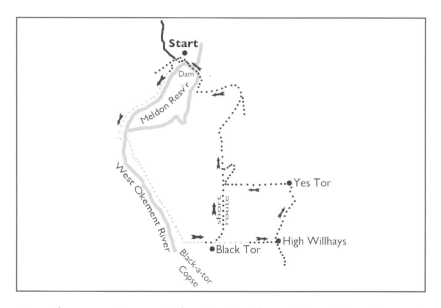

From the car park ascend the steps by the public toilet, go through the gate and cross the lane diagonally left. Pass through another gate onto a bridle path signposted to Sourton and Reservoir Walk. Ascend for 100 metres then turn left again signposted Reservoir Walk. The view of the reservoir to your left opens out and you continue along a scenic path that offers many vistas both across the water and to the open moorland beyond. As you reach the end of the reservoir enjoy the views ahead to Sourton Tors and Corn Ridge. Notice too the island in the reservoir, a haven for birds.

When you reach a gate turn left on the stony path, still on the Reservoir Walk and now heading downhill. About 200 metres along look out for steps descending to the left. At the bottom of these steps the path turns left through a gate and over an attractive bridge spanning the West Okement River. Pause here and admire your surroundings – a good spot for a picnic, weather permitting. Pick up the well-trodden path that traverses SSE across the meadow heading towards a rocky tor ahead – this is Black Tor. This can be a damp and marshy area, good for damselflies. Follow

*Bridge over the West Okement River*

the distinct track that rises from the meadow along the left side of the valley. Keep the river to your right and as the path begins to flatten out an area of woodland comes into view. This is Black-a-tor Copse and up to the left of this is Black Tor.

The terrain underfoot becomes quite rocky and, at times, testing – so take care. Keep along in the same direction towards the copse passing a granite enclosure on your right. Look out for ponies here, you have a good chance of spotting them. Beyond the rocks the area can again be quite damp and marshy (wear an orange hat!) so daggle your way carefully through this area still heading for the copse. Corn Ridge now rises to your right. Black-a-Tor Copse is one of three areas of ancient 'wild' woodland on Dartmoor, the other two being Wistman's Wood and Piles Copse. Full of lichen-encrusted oak trees and mossy boulders, tread lightly in this area. These are delicate habitats and are probably best left undisturbed, explored just with your eyes from the periphery. Once you reach the copse turn left and head up to the two distinct outcrops of Black Tor. There is a path through the bracken which is easy to miss, but the Tor, at 488 metres above sea level, isn't!

Get your breath back at Black Tor, enjoy another picnic and marvel at the views. Notice the path heading north along Longstone Hill. For those not wishing to explore the higher tors of Yes and High Willhays this is the path you want. For the more intrepid amongst you make a mental note of this path as you will be joining it later.

For the more adventurous route continue almost due east (100°) up the rising land until you find yourself on a clear path between the two granite-topped tors: Yes Tor – 619 metres (SX581901) and High Willhays – 621 metres (SX581892). This is just under a mile from Black Tor. Turn right (south) on the path ascending to High Willhays with its cairn. Wonder at the views – you are higher than anybody else in southern England!

From High Willhays return to the path, this time heading in a mostly northerly direction to the more visually dramatic Yes Tor with its trig point and a tall pole, very noticeable from afar. This is yet another good picnic site above the vast open spaces. On a clear day the distant hills of Exmoor can be seen away to the north east.

Leave Yes Tor and head down due west, ignoring any of the paths heading north from Yes Tor. Your route takes you through a pathless area of granite clitter so watch your step. If you stop and spare a glance around you the views are stunning. Glance to your right as you descend to see Meldon Quarry in the distance. The two distinct cragginesses of Black Tor will reappear to your left and you will be able to see the path across Longstone Hill, trodden earlier by the less daring. Pass through a line of well-spaced, red and white military range markers. About 300 metres beyond these on your westerly route you will meet the path from Black Tor at grid ref SX567901. Keep a sharp eye open as this often stony path occasionally becomes unreasonably indistinct. Turn right along this path, now heading north away from Black Tor.

Glance back as you follow this path. Yes Tor, to the right and behind you, is mighty and impressive. Meldon Quarry comes into view again, now ahead of you to the left. The path begins to drop and bears very slightly right. Another path comes in from the right, keep ahead on this clear route, descending and bearing left with the track. Meldon Viaduct can now be seen ahead.

Keep with this broad path as it continues to drop towards the reservoir, the dam is clearly visible below. Beyond the reservoir you can see our old friends, Corn Ridge and Sourton Tors. The path sweeps down, keep with it all the way to the reservoir (yet more picnic spots) where you turn right, with the fence on your left, to follow the path to the dam. Cross the water on this wonderful vantage point and at the far side turn left on the lane, then bear right, to arrive back at the car park.

### Meldon Reservoir and Viaduct

After 10 years of battling between the Water Board and conservation organisations, the dam across the West Okement River was constructed, and Meldon Reservoir, situated at around 270 metres above sea level, opened in 1972. The dam is 55 metres high and can hold back 300 million litres of water. The impact on the landscape was immense but the subsequent, newly-created landscape has its own beauty. During the walk you will see the 165 metres steel span of Meldon Viaduct in the distance. Built in 1870 to accommodate the railway, it closed less than 100 years later then re-opened in 2002 to become part of The Granite Way and National Cycle Network – Sustrans Route 27 crosses it.

*Walk 5*
## Trentishoe & the Heddon Valley

*This stunning route takes in a spectacular segment of the Exmoor coastline, an idyllic, wooded river valley and a famous hostelry popular with walkers, which provides hearty sustenance and quality beer. There are some steep ascents and descents and good footwear is essential as the paths can be rough in places.*

---

**Map:** OS Outdoor Leisure 9, Exmoor 1:25 000

**Start point:** Trentishoe Down Car Park. Grid ref: SS628480

**Distance:** 8.5 miles / 13.7km

**Parking:** Area set aside for free parking on NT headland just over a mile by road to the west of Trentishoe. There are various parking areas, select Trentishoe Down as indicated by grid reference above

**Refreshments:** The Hunters Inn in the Heddon Valley: 01598 763230

**Toilets:** At Hunters Inn and near The NT Shop in the Heddon Valley, otherwise trees

**Nearby places to stay:** Heddon's Gate Hotel: 01598 763481; Hunters Inn: 01598 763230

**Nearby places of interest:** Arlington Court (NT): 01271 850296; Lynton & Barnstaple Railway: 01598 763487

**Possible birds include:** Carrion crow, buzzard, chaffinch, chiffchaff, green woodpecker, grey wagtail, gulls, long tailed tit, peregrine, raven, skylark, whitethroat, willow warbler, wren

**Authors' tip:** Look out for a variety of mammals. On this walk we saw fox, deer and even a dolphin

---

Leave Trentishoe Down car park at the north east side diagonally opposite the vehicle access from the road. Pass between wooden benches and pick up the grassy path heading towards the coast. The magnificent spectacle of North Cleave and High Cliff lies ahead of you. Reach the coast path fingerpost and turn right heading east towards Heddon's Mouth. When the path eventually forks keep left signposted to Hunters Inn, 3 miles. Continue through footpath gates remembering to also admire the views behind you across Elwill Bay and to the woody coastline below.

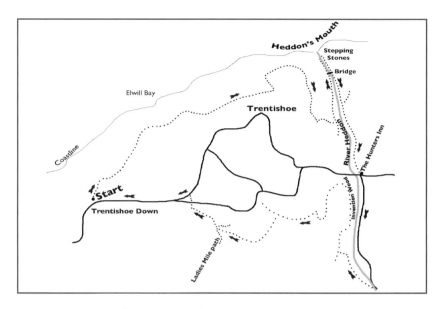

Continue along the coast path until another footpath gate (rather than a field gate) leads you into a field.

Continue on the coast path and at the next fingerpost go left ignoring the right turn towards Trentishoe Church. Continue round the headland with a dramatic rocky landscape ahead of you until you reach the Heddon Valley. The only option here is to turn sharp right but before you do take time out to relish the coastal and valley views. Continue inland along the rim of the Heddon Valley with views towards The Hunters Inn framed by wooded slopes. The path then descends steeply into the valley and can be shaly in places so take care.

Once you reach the valley floor turn left towards Heddon's Mouth. This is Heddon's Mouth Cleave and follows the River Heddon, on your right, all the way to the sea. Ignore any left or right turns on the way. At Heddon's Mouth linger a moment to savour the area before heading back inland, crossing the stepping stones (if possible) and taking the slightly higher rocky path. After wet

*Stepping stones in the Heddon Valley*

weather these stepping stones are often submerged, in which case you will need to cross by the bridge a little further back. Continue for approximately one mile to The Hunters Inn keeping the river on your right. The final stretch of the path enters the grounds of the Inn where you might be lucky to spot a peacock.

Rest awhile, partake of the excellent ale and vittles and seek out Winifred Paul whose photograph from 1930 hangs on the wall and who is granny to one of the authors.

After suitable refreshment, stagger out through the door and head straight along the road signposted Parracombe and Lynton passing the NT Shop on your left. About three quarters of a mile from the Inn you reach the attractive buildings of Mill Farm. Turn sharp right opposite here to join the footpath signposted to Hunters Inn and Heale. Cross the footbridge and go right with the footpath. Keep on this footpath with the river to your right. There

## The Hunters Inn

The original building on this site was burned down and rebuilt at the end of the 19thC. It has, over the decades, been the haunt of the glamorous and well-known as well as more regular folk. Not least amongst these is one of our grannies! James Clancy's grandmother, Winifred Paul, visited this Inn during the 1930s. Look out for her. A photograph of Winifred, alongside some not-then vintage cars, is hanging on the wall of the bar. More recently the Inn has been named CAMRA Pub of the Year 2009.

are some beautiful beech trees along this stretch. A fingerpost directs you straight on towards Trentishoe and Heale – the authors suggest you ignore the right turn back to The Hunters Inn. These things are sent to try us.

The next fingerpost directs you left up a path, still for Trentishoe and Heale and still ignoring the sign back to the Inn. You can have too much of a good thing and the hill ahead of you will work off any earlier over-indulgence. After quite a climb, pass through a gate and continue ahead as the path begins to level, then through another gate and walk ahead to join a stony track. Turn right downhill.

Continue down through the trees (Invention Wood) for some distance until you come to a broad junction. Turn right then immediately fork left signposted Trentishoe Mill and Rhydda Bank Cross. Walk past the picturesque Vention Cottage and cross another footbridge, then turn left. Continue ahead with the river on your left. At the next three-fingerpost, continue ahead signposted Trentishoe Mill and Heale and keep on in this direction until eventually you meet a tarmac path. Bear left along the tarmac for about 40 metres and then turn right up a distinct footpath. This leads you to the Ladies Mile and Trentishoe Down, although at the time of writing the sign telling you this had disappeared.

Climb up through the woodland to a cross-path. However tempting the picturesquely-named Ladies Mile might seem to right or left, your way is on up the steep hillside to Trentishoe and the coast path. Breather-stops are a good opportunity to enjoy the fabulous views behind you. This path winds up to the road, at which turn left. Soon you reach Holdstone Down Cross, the car park here is NOT the one from whence you started! Continue on the road towards Ilfracombe. This is also the Sustrans Cycle Route 51. Admire the views across the sea to Wales and after half a mile you will be back at your car.

*Evening Exmoor coastline*

*Walk 6*
# North Devon's Glorious Beaches

*This one is a must! The three beaches you visit are some of the most spectacular you will find. Renowned for their surf they offer a wonderful backdrop to this route at any time of year and at low tide provide for miles of sandy exploration, should you wish. Apart from a pretty stiff climb up from Saunton this is fairly comfortable walking with plenty of watering holes en route, though do check opening times out of season. When visibility is good, Lundy beckons you – a magical place for a different day.*

**Map:** OS Explorer 139, Bideford, Ilfracombe & Barnstaple 1:25 000

**Start point:** Putsborough. Grid ref SS447407

**Distance:** 8 miles / 12.9km

**Parking:** There is a car park at Putsborough Sands. Fee payable for half or whole days

**Refreshments:** Putsborough Sands Beach Café: 01271 890327; many options at Croyde and Saunton Sands

**Toilets:** Putsborough Sands, Croyde Bay, Saunton Sands

**Possible birds include:** Blackbird, buzzard, carrion crow, collared dove, cormorant, fulmar, goldfinch, greenfinch, gulls, house martin, house sparrow, jackdaw, kestrel, linnet, oystercatcher, peregrine, robin, shag, stonechat, swallow, woodpigeon

**Nearby places to stay:** Combas Farm, Putsborough: 01271 890398; Kittiwell House, Croyde: 01271 890247; The Saunton Sands Hotel: 01271 890212

**Nearby places of interest:** Lundy can be visited for a day trip as well as holidays: 01271 863636 / www.lundyisland.co.uk

**Authors' tip:** We recommend tea on the terrace at the Saunton Sands Hotel, the furthest point of the walk. There are glorious views over the beach from here – although they don't allow dogs on the premises

Leave the car park up the footpath just above the toilets and wind your way up the cliff. At the top pause and look back to get your bearings. You have climbed up from Putsborough and Woolacombe Sands. This is Morte Bay, the town of Woolacombe is on the other side of the bay and Morte Point juts out to sea. Turn right now to walk away from Morte Bay following the path with

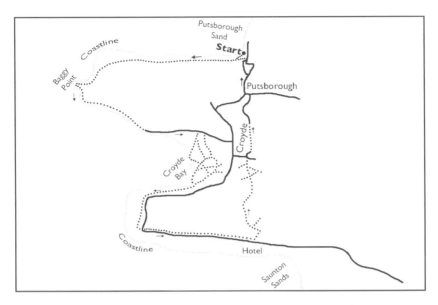

the sea to your right, this is the South West Coast Path and Tarka Trail above Napps Cliff. Lundy comes into view ahead of you out in the Bristol Channel. On a clear day you might be able to make out the tower of St. Helena's Church, the Old Light and, further to the north, the protuberance of Tibbetts, one of the holiday cottages on the island.

Follow the path and cross a stile which leads onto NT land around Baggy Point. In the summer look out for the delightful common blue butterfly along here. When you see a sign for Baggy Point ½ mile continue, and further on as you approach the headland, at a spot where the path bends left round a wall, you can see all three beaches at once, Woolacombe behind you, Croyde and Saunton ahead.

Soon you see the white triangulation pillar above Baggy Point. At the end of the wall a sign directs you right along the coast path down towards the sea. Take this and pass through a gate onto the stunning headland, popular with rock climbers, birdwatchers and

*The beach at Putsborough and Woolacombe*

semi-wild goats, as well as walkers. Just beyond the gate the coast path goes left, take it and head for Croyde Bay. When you leave the NT owned land look out for the memorial to Henry Williamson in the wall on the left. He authored *Tarka the Otter*, this path still being part of the Tarka Trail.

Continue on the lane through Croyde Bay, you are still on the coast path with its acorn waymarkers, and keep an eye open for a big, grey, rock-like structure on the left of the path which is actually the remains of a whale washed up on the beach in 1915. You pass the NT's Sandleigh Tea Room and Gardens on your left and shortly after this take the path right off the lane through a gap in the wall, which continues parallel to the road but keeps you away from cars for a stretch.

Just beyond here is a choice depending on whether or not you are accompanied by a dog. For the dog-free amongst you turn right at the next junction where you are signposted towards the beach and toilets. Beyond the beach café go onto the sand and just before two huts, one of which belongs to the RNLI, you will see a fingerpost directing you left along the coast path. Go left along the dunes at the back of the beach. There is quite a network of paths here so keep heading towards the far side of the beach. Cross a stream over a small bridge then turn right towards the beach to continue skirting along the back of the sand through the network of paths and dunes heading south until you join up at (*) below.

Those with canine companions can't follow the coast path onto the beach between May and September so the alternative is to continue along the main lane rather than turning right to the beach and toilets. Our Pandora took this route and wrote up the next bit of the walk, which is pretty impressive when you see her toenails. So, dogs must continue along the main lane to take the next right turn by the telephone box, there is a footpath marker on the gate. Walk through the holiday chalets on the main path, which is all public footpath, heading in the direction of the sea. Leave the site through a gate with another yellow arrow and walk ahead to cross a footbridge. Beyond this, bear diagonally left across the grass to the far corner, leaving this grassy area through a gap and then along a path. This leads you in about 30 metres to a three-way fingerpost. Go 90° right here (as opposed to right back on yourself). This path leads to the back corner of the beach to meet the dogless (*). Skirt the beach for a few metres to leave the sand up the clearly-signed coast path.

This leads to another very short stretch of beach and then to steps up to a fingerpost. Turn right here towards Braunton (those requiring toilets can head inland for a few metres to more facilities at this point). This path goes round the headland to give views of Saunton Sands, then heads uphill to meet the lane. Go left along the lane for about 70 metres, being cautious as you will meet traffic here, then turn right up the footpath which winds its way along the cliffs towards Saunton Sands Hotel. There are fabulous views from up here and you might see the RAF Air Sea Rescue Helicopter carrying out exercises on this vast beach.

Eventually you reach a sign indicating that you should go right for Saunton and its various amenities, which is a nice option if it fits in with your plans. Otherwise turn left here towards Croyde and cross the stile, ascending steeply. When you reach a stile at the top of some steps, which crosses into a field, walk ahead to the fingerpost. From here look behind at the remarkable view of Braunton Burrows, the largest sand dune system in the UK, a National Nature Reserve and a UNESCO biosphere reserve. It's very impressive.

From the fingerpost follow the sign towards Croyde, 1 mile. You will see another fingerpost ahead on the skyline so aim for this and pass through the gate, still following the public footpath to Croyde as it wends its way through several fields. After a particularly impressive stile bear right through the field as directed by the yellow arrow and the series of waymark posts. Cross the next two

### Lundy

Three miles long by just over half a mile wide this island has a colourful history despite its small size. Evidence of occupation harks back to Neolithic times. Owned by the Marisco family in the 13th C., after whom the tavern is named, it has also been the haunt of pirates and, during the 18th C., the unofficial 'residence' of deported convicts. The Harman family owned it during the early 20thC. and in 1969 sold it to Jack Hayward who gave the island to The National Trust, the present owners. Lundy's holiday accommodation is administered by the Landmark Trust and it makes for a beautiful destination – a glorious place for bird watching, rock climbing, walking and diving amongst many other attractions. 'Lund-e' is old Norse for 'puffin island' and although the puffin population is now quite minimal you may still be lucky enough to see them in spring off the west coast.

stiles in quick succession and continue to descend along the tree-lined path. At a three-way junction take the option ahead (not left) towards Croyde, through a kissing gate. This is Down Lane and leads to a gate onto a concrete track, with the picturesque name of Milkaway Lane. After about 20 metres the track bends left but you go right for another 20 metres, then keep left as the track forks, walking through trees.

This path descends to a road, turn left for a short distance and just in front of the Manor House Inn turn right to follow a small road past a car park on your left. This road soon bends left and passes Millers Brook on your right, and the lovely Kittiwell House on your left. Beyond here take the public byway which eventually leads you past the pretty gardens of Combas Farm. Continue ahead, ignoring a track which comes in from your left. When you reach the road turn left, and follow it as it bends right and back to your car at Putsborough Sands.

*Baggy Point*

*Air Sea Rescue rehearsals at Croyde (note Lundy Island in distance)*

*Walk 7*
# Exotic East Portlemouth

*Aside from the steep path from the car park, including over 100 steps, this is actually relatively easy walking. This is a walk for blue-sky days, which abounds with little coves and inlets and some of the county's most beautiful beaches. Salcombe estuary is a simply wonderful place to start this walk which then continues along glorious coastline before returning along picturesque inland paths.*

**Map**: OS Explorer Outdoor Leisure 20, South Devon 1:25 000

**Start point**: East Portlemouth. Grid ref SX746386

**Distance**: 4½ miles / 7.2km

**Parking**: There is an area set aside for car parking at East Portlemouth, high above the estuary overlooking the spectacular view. An honesty box raises funds for the Village Hall. If this parking area is full there is an alternative NT car park at Mill Bay (SX741381) which is more expensive and shortens the walk

**Refreshments**: The Gara Rock Hotel, East Portlemouth (re-opening end of 2011): 01548 842342; The Millbrook Inn, South Pool: 01548 531581; Venus Café in East Portlemouth by the ferry steps: 01548 843558. If you take the ferry boat across to the other side of the estuary there are numerous places to eat in and around Salcombe including The Ferry Inn where you disembark: 01548 844000

**Toilets**: East Portlemouth, near the Venus Café; Mill Bay, by the car park

**Possible birds include**: Chiffchaff, cormorant, gannet, goldfinch, skylark, swallow, woodpigeon, wren

**Nearby places to stay**: Gara Rock Hotel, East Portlemouth: 01548 842342; Salcombe Harbour Hotel, Salcombe: 01548 844444; Tides Reach Hotel, South Sands, Salcombe: 01548 843466. There are numerous other B&Bs on both sides of the estuary

**Nearby places of interest**: Overbecks (NT): 01548 842893

**Authors' tip**: Venus Café is perfect on a sunny day: sit back with a cuppa tea and immerse yourself in the ambience and boat-life on the estuary

Emerge from car, select a bench and absorb the views over the estuary. If you don't get any further today this alone was worth the trip. The car park leads to a grassy slope and thence to a gate with a narrow tarmac footpath beyond. There is a sign pointing down here to passageway and the public footpath for Salcombe,

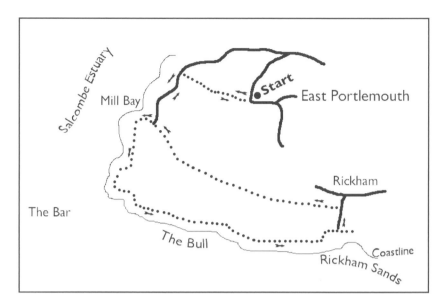

½m. Descend the steps and turn right for your first stop at the Venus Café, a wonderful spot at which to enjoy refreshments with a backdrop of Salcombe across the water and a hive of boating activity in the foreground. The public toilets are beyond the café.

From the Venus Café turn right along the lane, passing the access to the ferry on your right. This can be a treat for later, time permitting. Follow the lane past lovely houses as far as Mill Bay which is the alternative parking place. Those who have left their car here will start the walk from this point. Find the three-fingerpost which directs you right for Gara Rock, 2½ miles, on the acorn way-marked coast path and follow this into woodland.

When the path forks keep right ignoring the top path for Gara Rock. Enjoy tempting glimpses through the trees of golden sands and turquoise waters. When the path forks again your route climbs left through the trees. We would, however, recommend a short detour along the right hand path to admire the enticing beach that awaits you. A fine stop for a picnic and a paddle. Return to the

*Down the Salcombe Estuary*

coast path and continue. Across the estuary you will see the beaches of South Sands to the left and North Sands to the right – the latter sporting the amusingly-named 'Winking Prawn' a tempting beach café. You will also see the impressive headlands of Sharp Tor and Bolt Head. Keep following the coast path signs (acorn symbol).

The path curves to the left away from the estuary, and sea views to your right could yield the occasional seal on the rocks below you or, if you're lucky, a dolphin swimming by. Eventually the path ascends to a meeting of ways – don't take the top path to Mill Bay. Continue ahead towards the little white, thatched lookout building that you'll see on top of the cliff. Before you reach this there is a right fork (coast path) which takes you to the attractive beach of Rickham Sands – highly recommended. After a rest and a snack on the beach retrace your steps and join the distinct path up towards Gara Rock and the white lookout that we saw earlier.

At the meeting of ways you have two options for Mill Bay. Take the shorter 1¼ mile route with the Gara Rock Hotel and Apartments to your right. It's worth visiting the white lookout on the left which can be reached along a little windy path for the views it affords over Rickham Sands and the surrounding coastline.

Proceed along a narrow tarmac lane in a northerly direction away from Gara Rock. After approximately 200 metres take the footpath on your left towards Mill Bay, 1 mile. Follow this fenced path between fields. This soon becomes tree-lined. At a meeting of ways descend some steps and cross to a gate with a blue bridleway sign. Continue through this gate in the same direction.

For those dendrologists amongst you a real treat awaits. Ancient giants of pollarded lime trees guide you on your return to Mill Bay. They are a remarkable sight. On entering the Mill Bay car park you now have two choices. You can either retrace your steps along the lane towards the Venus Café or, if tide permits, it's a pleasant diversion to make your way back along the sandy beaches as far as the ferry pontoon where you can ascend the steps back to the

### East Portlemouth Beaches

The tucked-away beaches at East Portlemouth have long been a favourite of the authors. Privately-owned and dog-friendly all year round, they are an extremely beautiful part of the coastline. On those all-too-rare, blue-sky summer days you'd be forgiven for thinking you  were in some far-away, exotic location. The whole atmosphere of this area is steeped in the essence of 'al fresco'. If time allows take the ferry over to Salcombe. This is not only a cost-effective method of getting on the water but it's a lovely way to approach this colourful and vibrant Devon town.

lane. If you take this latter option be aware, depending on the level of the tide, you may have some rock scrambling to do. Once back on the lane you are left with the final climb up the steps back to the top car park.

*Lime avenue*

*Waterfall, West Okement River (Meldon & the High Tors)*

The view from Black Tor (Meldon & the High Tors)

Branscombe bloom (Branscombe & the Hooken Undercliff)

*Newton Creek (Noss Mayo & the Warren)*       *Goats in Valley of Rocks (Little Switzerland)*

*Heddon's Mouth (Trentishoe & the Heddon Valley)*

*Looking west towards Salcombe Estuary (Exotic East Portlemouth)*

*Starehole Bay (Bolt Head & Soar Mill Cove)*

*Looking across the estuary to Salcombe (Exotic East Portlemouth)*

*Yealscombe Wood (The Doone Valley)*
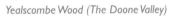

*Tavy Cleave from Ger Tor (Tavy Cleave)*

*Devil's Kitchen (Tavy Cleave)*

*Doone Valley sheep*

*Bantham Boathouse (Bigbury-on-Sea)*

*Putsborough (North Devon's Glorious Beaches)*

*Saunton Sands (North Devon's Glorious Beaches)*

*Overlooking Soar Mill Cove (Bolt Head & Soar Mill Cove)*

*Walk 8*
# The Doone Valley

*This is a very picturesque route which initially takes you along the Doone Valley, made famous in R.D. Blackmore's novel. The return part of the route is across wild, high moorland. As always, good footwear is a must.*

**Map:** OS Outdoor Leisure 9, Exmoor 1:25 000

**Start point:** Malmsmead Car Park. Grid ref: SS792478

**Distance:** 6.5 miles / 10.5km

**Parking:** There is a very reasonably-priced pay and display car park in Malmsmead adjacent to the Doone Valley Camp Site

**Refreshments:** The Buttery Riverside Bar and Café, Malmsmead: 01598 741106

**Toilets:** Situated in the car park at Malmsmead

**Possible birds include:** Bullfinch, buzzard, carrion crow, chaffinch, chiffchaff, grey heron, grey wagtail, kestrel, mallard, siskin, swallow, wren

**Nearby places to stay:** The Blue Ball Inn: 01598 741263; Doone Valley Camp Site: 01598 741267

**Nearby places of interest:** Lynmouth and Lynton and all their attractions

**Authors' tip:** For those who enjoy horse riding there are some good local trekking centres and this is a lovely, alternative way to enjoy the valley

**Note: Be aware: the return section of this route is across open moorland, so a map and compass are a must – and clear weather conditions**

Leave the car park and turn left, quickly reaching a junction of lanes. Opposite you will see a gate with an honesty box. This leads you across private land which the owner is happy to permit, for a small fee. We recommend this start, but if you prefer to walk up the lane to the right for about ¼ mile you will find access to a bridleway, signposted Badgworthy Valley, ½ mile, which will eventually lead you to (*) below.

For those paying the fee and taking the first option, walk ahead on the path. The river on your left is Badgworthy Water and at this point it is the boundary between Devon and Somerset. You are heading south. Soon you see the farm buildings of Cloud Farm

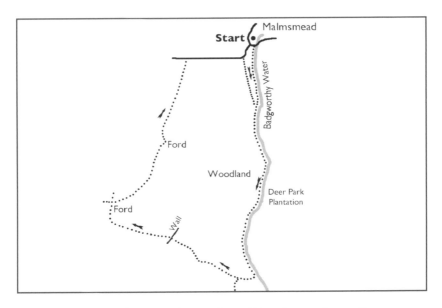

ahead of you to the left. The path will lead you through a gate to cross a small stream (less small, after heavy rain!). From this point walk ahead across the grass to a fingerpost. A bridle path comes in here from the right along which those who avoided paying will approach (*). Now keep ahead in the same direction along the bridle path, ignoring the left turn across the footbridge to Oare Church. You are heading for the Doone Valley.

Soon you will pass a memorial stone erected in 1969 by the Lorna Doone Committee to the memory of R.D. Blackmore. As the path forks keep left to continue near the river, although the paths soon merge again. In the summer this area is heaving with swallows. Less than ½ mile from the footbridge the path enters Yealscombe then Badgworthy Woods, keep ahead on the main bridle path ignoring any tracks up into the trees. After some way through the woods you will reach a river crossing called Sir Hugh's Ride. This is a permitted bridle path and the river can be crossed here on horseback, but your way lies ahead without crossing, keeping the river to your left.

*Malmsmead*

About 100 metres beyond Sir Hugh's Ride the path emerges from the trees. Keep ahead on the same bridle path, ignoring the broad track sweeping round to the right. The river is now slightly further away to your left but soon curves in again and you are once more walking amongst trees. Soon you cross a footbridge over a tributary stream. The area here is very pretty and worth a glance, but then continue ahead as before.

The path eventually climbs a little but still keep the river to your left, passing occasional blue bridle path markers. The view opens up across the valley. This is all Doone Country, to the left you will see the huge, treeless mound of Deer Park. About ½ mile after you have left the trees the bridle path takes a distinct right turn. This area is the site of a medieval village. Your route follows this bend, although it is worth first visiting the delightful area down to the left on the permitted path which leads to the river from which you have good views in both directions along the Doone Valley.

Back at the bend you will soon see a way-marker post showing that your way leads to Brendon Common. Left is to Tom's Hill, which you ignore. The watercourse which is now down to your left is Hoccombe Coombe. Keep on the blue-marked bridle path as it takes you in a generally north westerly direction across moorland (although the path bends a bit you are on a bearing of approximately 310°).

About one mile from the right hand bend and way-marker, pass through a gate with a fingerpost which reassuringly indicates that you are still on the bridle path (SS781452). There are superb views from here. Keep on the clear track for another ¾ mile until the path descends to cross Lankcombe Ford. Beyond here head up the hill on the right hand of the two distinct paths. A sign here requests that you keep to this, the main track which heads very slightly east of north from the ford. This is a moorland conservation area.

You soon see a fingerpost ahead at a crossing of ways. From here turn right to Malmsmead, 2¾m, on the clear track enjoying more fabulous views. About ¾ mile from the cross ways you will see a gate on your right and the track takes a distinct left turn (SS780465). Go with this. There is a ford here after wet weather but

**Lorna Doone**
First published in the latter part of the 19ᵗʰ century R.D. Blackmore's novel of this name is set in the area of Badgworthy Water during the 18ᵗʰ C. and draws on fragments of historical fact which are woven into the fiction. The main character, John Ridd, falls in love with the eponymous heroine but, inevitably, all does not run smoothly since she belongs to the notorious and marauding Doone family who murdered his father. This doesn't diminish his ardour and after much skirmishing and violence things work out in the end. The romance has blended with this beautiful part of the moor to become part of the folklore and you will see much evidence of the Doones and the Ridds in this area.

it is often dry and invisible. Follow this track, the sea eventually comes into view ahead of you and to the right. Once you reach the lane turn right and follow it back down to Malmsmead and your car.

*The Doone Valley*

# Bolt Head & Soar Mill Cove

*From the initial views over the Salcombe Estuary to the rocky drama of this section of the South Hams coastline this route is simply stunning. There are a few steep inclines and some precipitous paths so caution, as always, is advised. Otherwise this is fairly simple walking. There is the tempting option of a refreshing paddle at Soar Mill Cove.*

---

**Map:** OS Explorer Outdoor Leisure 20, South Devon 1:25 000

**Start point:** Footpath adjacent to The NT's Overbeck's entrance. Grid ref SX728374

**Distance:** 9.5 miles / 15.3km

**Parking:** Parking in this area is limited. An option is to head for The Tides Reach Hotel at South Sands or, with luck, on-lane parking below the start point near Overbeck's. There is a larger alternative car park alongside The Winking Prawn Beach Café at North Sands, but this does extend the walk somewhat

**Refreshments:** Soar Mill Cove Hotel, Soar Mill Cove, Nr Salcombe: 01548 561566; The Winking Prawn Beach Café & BBQ, North Sands, Salcombe: 01548 842326; many options in the town of Salcombe itself

**Toilets:** Located at South Sands and North Sands. Nothing en route unless you're eating/drinking at Soar Mill Cove Hotel

**Possible birds include:** Blackbird, blue tit, buzzard, cormorant, goldfinch, house sparrow, kestrel, linnet, magpie, meadow pipit, peregrine, raven, shag, stonechat, swallow, wheatear, whitethroat, willow warbler, woodpigeon, wren, yellowhammer

**Possible butterflies include:** Brimstone, common blue, red admiral

**Nearby places to stay:** Higher Rew Caravan and Camping Park, Malborough: 01548 842681; Soar Mill Cove Hotel, Soar Mill Cove, Nr Salcombe: 01548 561566; South Sands Hotel, South Sands, Salcombe: 01548 859000; Tides Reach Hotel, South Sands, Salcombe: 01548 843466; many options in the town of Salcombe itself

**Nearby places of interest:** Overbeck's (NT), Sharpitor, Salcombe: 01548 842893

**Authors' tip:** The Soar Mill Cove Hotel is quite a smart place to break for lunch – and boasts a Bollinger Bar, which, of course, we wouldn't recommend while you're walking!

---

You begin the walk at the exotic palm-tree-lined entrance to the NT property of Overbeck's. As you face the gate you'll notice a footpath to the right signposted to Bolt Head. Proceed along here

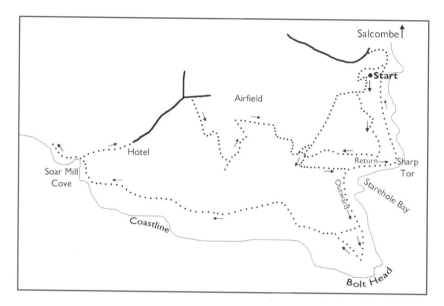

and shortly after you'll see a fingerpost pointing left for Sharp Tor, Starehole and Bolt Head. Take this path ascending some steps. Fabulous views across the Salcombe Estuary soon become apparent.

The coast path bears right leaving the Estuary and continues with the sea to your left. When you reach a fingerpost ignore the right turn to Soar Mill Cove and Bolberry and instead continue ahead to Starehole and Bolt Head. Go through a gate and at the next fingerpost go left, again signed for Starehole and Bolt Head. This leads you down towards the sea at Starehole Bay along a path through the delightfully named Starehole Bottom! This broad grassy track leads down to another fingerpost at which point you have Bolt Head, Soar Mill Cove and Bolberry all signposted right. This is just the reassurance you need as each of these locations is on your route.

Explore round the headland of Bolt Head continuing with the sea on your left to return and reunite with the main coast path. At Bolt

*Starehole Bay*

Head Cross there is a crossways fingerpost, continue ahead on the coast path through the gate towards Soar Mill Cove, 2½m. When you reach a gate to the left of the track proceed through this to continue on the coast path. You'll notice an acorn symbol on the reverse of this gate. At the time of writing there is a wire fence on your right. Indeed, whenever you have options keep on the coast path to Soar Mill Cove and savour the fabulous views that this stretch of coastline has to offer.

The path eventually descends to Soar Mill Cove. Before exploration of this wonderful dog-friendly beach we recommend continuing up the path towards Bolberry Down until you reach a viewpoint by a bench. Glorious views of the coast and back towards the cove can be had from here. Also, whilst here, it's worth making a mental note of a single-storey building at the top of the right-hand valley behind the cove. This is the Soar Mill Cove Hotel which is on your route.

Retrace your steps to the beach for a well-earned paddle and then head inland along the aforementioned right-hand valley towards the Soar Mill Cove Hotel. You can reach the correct path by emerging from the beach, turning right across a wooden footbridge and going through a gate. The sea at this stage is down to your right. Once through the gate immediately turn left along the trodden path heading inland.

The Soar Mill Cove Hotel is a welcome stop should you need refreshing. We did!

Leave the hotel on the road adjacent to the car park and head uphill. After 300 metres you meet a collection of buildings and a footpath right. Ignore this and continue 100 metres to another collection of houses with a postbox in the wall. This is Higher Soar Farm. Walk past these buildings and pick up another footpath right leading you down to the coast path. This is signed to Middle Soar, ½m. Initially you walk through a private garden to a gate with a yellow arrow, so please respect the privacy of the owners.

Continue ahead to the next gate and through the field ahead with the boundary on your left – you're heading back towards the sea at this point with a sea view also to your right. At the end of the field follow the yellow arrow left through a gap in the hedge to cross a short distance to a waymarker post where you'll find a yellow arrow pointing you right. You can see the roof of a house ahead of you, this is Middle Soar. Keep straight through this field for about 350 metres and then you'll notice a yellow arrow ahead and slightly left of you. This points you over a stile with the house still in view. Beyond the stile you're bearing slightly left through the field heading for another guiding waymarker post. Middle Soar is now to your right (at the time of writing earthworks were being carried out near here. If the route is altered in any way from our description, waymark arrows should guide you).

Soon you meet a track and the waymarker post with yellow arrows gives you a choice. Turn left along the track, you are heading inland at this point. Go through a gate and turn left along a tarmac lane. About 150 metres along you emerge into a car park where there is an information board about the RAF at Bolt Head and Hope Cove. You'll notice a footpath fingerpost to the right. Turn right here heading alongside the airfield to Salcombe 3m, Overbeck's 2m, Sharp Tor 2m. The NT sign shortly afterwards indicates you're entering East Soar Farm. This is nice easy walking along a gravelly track with a tall mast on the left.

The track bends right after the airfield where you'll come across a three-way fingerpost. Ignore the option to go left and continue ahead on the track signposted to Sharp Tor 1m, Starehole 1m, Bolt Head 1½m. This track leads you past the stone buildings of East Soar Farm on your right. Beyond the end barn you'll see another fingerpost sign. Go right here through a kissing gate signed for Sharp Tor ¾m, Starehole ¾m, Bolt Head 1¼m. There's a short stretch through this field to another gate with the field's boundary

**Overbeck's and Airfields**
The NT property of Overbeck's, once the home of the unorthodox scientist Otto Overbeck who bought it in 1928, is an Edwardian house built on the site of an earlier Victorian building. Before the arrival of Otto it was known as Sharpitor House. Some of the rooms are open to the public and contain the fascinating Overbeck's Museum. The remainder of the building houses a Youth Hostel. The lush, sub-tropical gardens are well-worth a visit. Otto bequeathed the property to the Trust in 1937.
The RAF presence in the Bolt Head area dates back to World War II. The airfield at Bolt Head was built in 1940, after the harvest, and was operational from 1941. It served as a busy satellite airfield to RAF Exeter. It now has just a single runway and is occasionally used for private light aircraft. A peaceful area, it's hard to imagine how it once thrummed with spitfires and typhoons.

to your right. Go through this next gate and continue in the same direction along a trodden path. You're following the same line as per the previous fingerpost and soon you're back to the coast and amongst all the spectacular scenery again.

As you walk over the brow of the hill head down to a fingerpost beyond. Leave this field across another stile and turn right for Starehole. This section means a tiny amount of retracing from earlier to enable us to take in Sharp Tor. At the bottom go through the gate and ahead of you you'll notice the fingerpost which points you left towards Bolt Head and Starehole. Go down here. This is Starehole Bottom again, we liked the name so much we thought we'd bring you here twice! This time at the base of the path when you meet a three-way fingerpost you want to turn left signed for Overbeck's, Tor Woods, Salcombe. Go through the gate here and head up a spectacular path to the towering granite of Sharp Tor.

*Soar Mill Cove*

The sea is on your right and there are views across to Prawle Point – the southernmost point of Devon. Tread carefully on this path as it is a little rocky underfoot.

As it rounds the rock face you are greeted by the serenity of the Salcombe Estuary again. This path eventually becomes tree-lined. At the end of the footpath you'll see another fingerpost called Overbeck's. Where you turn here is dependent on where you've parked your car. Head left to visit Overbeck's, or right towards The Tides Reach and The Winking Prawn Beach Café.

*En route to Soar Mill Cove*          *Bolt Head*

# Bigbury-on-Sea & Burgh Island

*The backdrop of Burgh Island provides a dramatic view for the start point of this walk. The route has a few ascents but is otherwise comfortable walking despite a brief muddy stretch. The opportunity to visit the beach at Cockleridge Ham and stroll along to see the Bantham Boathouse when the tide permits is an added attraction. Burgh Island can be visited by walking across at low tide or by taking the unique 'sea tractor'.*

**Map:** OS Explorer Outdoor Leisure 20, South Devon 1:25 000

**Start point:** Bigbury-on-Sea. Grid ref: SX651442

**Distance:** 6.5 miles / 10.5km

**Parking:** Bigbury-on-Sea Beach Car Park. There is an alternative 'economy' car park which you pass as you enter the village which is good but doesn't have the facilities of the main car park

**Refreshments:** The Pilchard Inn, Burgh Island: 01548 810514; Royal Oak Inn, Bigbury: 01548 810313; Venus Café, Bigbury-on-Sea Car Park: 01803 712648

**Toilets:** Situated in the beach car park at Bigbury-on-Sea

**Possible birds include:** Buzzard, chaffinch, cormorant, goldfinch, great tit, house sparrow, linnet, little egret, magpie, pied wagtail, robin, rook, song thrush, swallow, woodpigeon, yellowhammer

**Possible butterflies include:** Common blue, gatekeeper, green veined white, holly blue, large white, peacock, red admiral, small tortoiseshell

**Nearby places to stay:** For a real splurge, Burgh Island Hotel: 01548 810514. B&Bs in Bigbury are quite sparse but there are plenty of self-catering options, Hexdown Barns being a particularly lovely one: 01548 811131

**Nearby places of interest:** Burgh Island

**Authors' tip:** The best way to approach this village is along the tidal road from Aveton Gifford – a quite remarkable way to start your day. If you plan to do this bear in mind that it isn't passable at high tide, so check tide times

Within the car park you will see a fingerpost for the coast path which directs you back to the car park entrance. Just outside the entrance, on your right, a yellow arrow points you along a little path above the beach with the road on your left. Take this and descend steps to a small metalled path leading to the beach. Turn left here away from the beach, you will see the acorn coast path waymarker. 50 metres along go right to follow the fingerpost which directs you

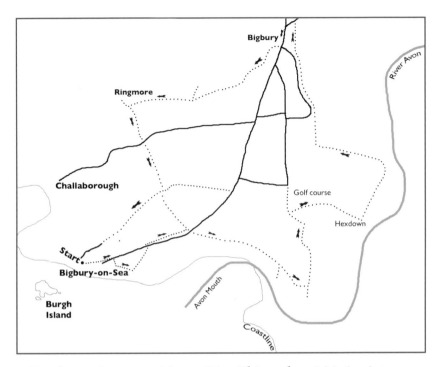

to Bantham, via seasonal ferry, 1½m. This path quickly leads to open ground with the sea to your right and Burgh Island behind. You will see a cottage ahead, just before this follow the footpath arrow which directs you left, following the garden wall on your right.

This path leads past houses (you will also see the 'economy' car park down on your left) to meet a road. Turn left and cross the road to enter the aforementioned car park. Turn right after the entrance to follow a permissive path up through several fields with the boundary and road on your right. Eventually this path leads out to cross the road again, you will see a fingerpost in the hedge signed for Bantham. Cross the road and continue ahead with the farmhouse on your right and farm buildings on your left. Just beyond the buildings you will see an acorned gate and fingerpost, pass through and continue with the fence on your right – there are gorgeous views here over the beach and across to Burgh Island.

*The River Avon near Bigbury-on-Sea*

Follow the fence as it eventually bends right and continues down towards the water – a waymarker directs you.

At the bottom of the fence cross a stile and continue to The Old Boathouse. Just past here you find a sign indicating that you are in the area of Cockleridge Ham. If the tide permits this is the point at which it's worth visiting the beach and walking along to see the picturesque Bantham Boathouse on the other side of the water. Once back at the sign for Cockleridge Ham continue on the path to emerge at a second sign about the Ham. A very weathered fingerpost directs you across the area behind the beach for about 100 metres to another post where the acorn and arrow directs you left down to a sunken path. Follow this and after 100 metres you emerge to see another fingerpost, this time sending you left towards Bigbury, 1¾m. You are now heading inland and up steps. Cross the stile at the top and continue up the field with its boundary on your right.

At the top of the field go left as the arrow directs, keeping the fence on your right, to leave via a gate where another arrow directs you right up a grass and tarmac track. This goes gently uphill to emerge onto a golf course. Signs direct you here and walkers are well guided. The path bends left and ahead you will see a fingerpost on the skyline. At the post ignore the left turn back to Bigbury-on-Sea and continue ahead through the golf course. More lovely views from here, if it's safe to raise your head. The next junction is reached quickly, keep a lookout for a fingerpost on your left. When you reach it, go right on the Avon Estuary Walk, the sign for this is a white heron on a blue background. Cross the cattle grid and enter the land of Hexdown.

At Hexdown Farm you may be lucky enough to find Kate and Anna's Shop – a delightful stall selling jam, posies and other produce. Go past the farm, cross the cattle grid and bear right on the track round garages to pass barn conversions on your left, these are lovely holiday lets. There are good views across the Avon on your right. Pass through the gate and continue as directed by the arrow, bearing right at the fork to head back down towards the water. Continue through another gate and continue with the fence on your right.

Descend to a metalled path where an Avon Estuary Walk sign directs you left along this drive. On your right you soon pass a house called Greenwell beyond which more glimpses of the estuary are waiting for you. Your route is soon flanked by some spectacularly-limbed and ancient trees and a little later the farm of Lincombe. As the lane heads up to meet the road, about 20 metres before you reach it, you will see a gap on your right leading to a permissive path. Go through here and continue with the hedge on your left, to avoid walking along the road. Ahead you can see the beckoning spire of Bigbury Church.

Keep on, passing through another field, still on the Avon Estuary Walk. At the next gate continue on the footpath ahead, don't take the right hand option. Follow the left hand boundary of this field until you find the exit of the footpath on your left, with stone steps descending to the lane. Turn left along the lane to the junction, left at the junction and then left again into The Royal Oak.

Post-pub, continue along the road past the shop to the next right turn, about 50 metres beyond the pub, at which there is a footpath sign to Ringmore, 1¼m. Mariners Cottage is on your right as you enter this path. Pass another cottage on your right, where it appears that you are walking through their beautifully-kept garden. Keep ahead on the grassy path, which soon becomes tree-lined. Cross the stile and continue ahead through the field. Leave the field over a stile, turning right and after a few metres turn left after a stream. The path beyond here can be a bit damp! After the next gate walk up to the fence as directed by the arrow and

**Burgh Island**

This tiny, tidal island is nowadays dominated by its smart hotel, but it is thought that a monastery was once situated here. Known originally as St. Michael's Island, it later became Borough Island, and this was eventually corrupted to Burgh. After the Dissolution the life of the island was dominated by pilchard fishing, hence the name of its 14ᵗʰ C. Inn. In more recent history, the island inspired some of Agatha Christie's novels and was also used as a film location. Other luminaries who have stayed here over the years reputedly include Edward and Mrs. Simpson, The Beatles and Noel Coward. At high tide the hotel operates the remarkable 'sea tractor' to move people on and off the island.

*View across Avon Mouth to Bantham Sands*

continue through the field with a fence on your left, hedge boundary to your right.

At the next fingerpost which gives you the option of going right over a footbridge, don't, but instead keep ahead on the track and soon you will reach a kissing gate to your right with another arrow. Follow this arrow to the next gate where yet another arrow points you diagonally right up towards the top corner of the field. About 10 metres down from the top corner cross the stile and continue through the next field, the top boundary is to your right. At the end of the field you will find a fingerpost – you can see the roof of End House over the hedge in front of you. Turn left and go down the field, boundary on your right. At the bottom, pass through the kissing gate and continue on the clear path. This soon enters trees, wind through on the well-trodden path to cross a stile and attractive stone footbridge, then continue up through the next field with the boundary on your left. Should you need to pause for breath going up here there are some nice views behind back to End House. Challaborough Bay Holiday Park is down to your right as you climb.

At the top of the field emerge onto a lane, cross over, bearing right, to cross another footpath stile. Go straight ahead and as you go over the brow of the hill you will see below you a collection of gates. Head down towards them. Once through these continue as directed by the arrows up through the two fields beyond, the boundary to your right. Then through the next gate, and continue up to the fingerpost on the skyline. Here take the right hand option to Bigbury-on-Sea, ½m. You are now heading downhill towards the sea and Burgh Island. Keep on this clear path until it emerges onto the road between houses. Follow the road and it will deliver you back to the area of the car park.

# Tavy Cleave

*We have many favourite walks and this is another one. Despite the challenge of the terrain we feel this is a route not to be missed. It requires no lane walking, just glorious open moorland, superlative views and waterside paths which can be marshy, so stout footwear is needed. The final part of the route is a lovely, gentle way to round off the trek. Fabulous.*

## Important information

There are two salient points to consider before you start this walk. It is a glorious route but some of the terrain is tricky as there is a stretch of bouldering along the return journey which is quite challenging. We managed perfectly well with Pandora the dog and a gammy ankle, but be prepared for a bit of scrambling. Some of this is near the water's edge, so after times of heavy rain you may have to pick your way through higher up. As with most walks, it's probably advisable to have company. Visibility can change rapidly in this area. The walk should not be attempted without a compass and map and the ability to use both. Additionally the army train regularly in this area (Willsworthy Range) so do ensure you check the following website before setting out: www.dartmoor-ranges.co.uk/index.html Alternatively the firing programme is available on: 0800 458 4868. During the walk you will see subtle evidence of army occupation. Another useful site which gives tips for moorland treks is: www.tourbytor.co.uk/equip_walk.php

**Map:** OS Outdoor Leisure 28, Dartmoor 1:25 000

**Start point:** Lanehead car parking area. Grid ref SX537823

**Distance:** 4¾ miles / 7.6km

**Parking:** At Lanehead there is a parking area marked clearly on the map

**Refreshments:** The Elephant's Nest, Horndon: 01822 810273

**Toilets:** None en route

**Possible birds include:** Blackbird, goldfinch, great spotted woodpecker, house sparrow, meadow pipit, raven, redstart, ring ouzel, skylark, swallow, wheatear, wren

**Nearby places to stay:** The Elephant's Nest, Horndon: 01822 810273; Glebe End B&B, Peter Tavy: 01822 810696

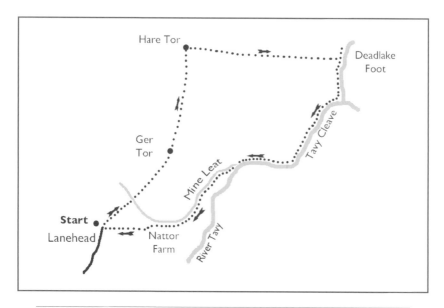

---

**Nearby places of interest:** Lydford Gorge (NT): 01822 820320; Tavistock and its attractions

**Authors' tip:** The nearby beauty spots of Lydford Gorge (NT) and Brent Tor are well-worth visiting if you have time. Lydford Gorge is famous for its spectacular White Lady and Devil's Cauldron waterfalls. Brent Tor's views from the summit are well worth the effort

---

At the car park look up to the north east and you can see the rocky outcrop of Ger Tor ¾ mile away. From the north east corner of the car park there is a distinct path heading towards this tor so seek this and go along it. Ahead of you a gate can be seen, aim for this as it leads onto a bridge which crosses the Mine Leat. Look out for roaming Dartmoor ponies, often with foals afoot during spring and summer.

Beyond the leat continue uphill towards Ger Tor. At times this path is indistinct, but the tor, with its mast, shouldn't be, so keep it in your sights as you walk towards the north east. This stretch can be damp underfoot but becomes increasingly rocky as you approach the tor so watch your step and take care of your

*Looking from Hare Tor towards Ger Tor*

ankles. As you continue to climb you will see Tavy Cleave down on your right.

Once you achieve Ger Tor you are over 430 metres above sea level and this is an area worth exploring. You may find the little stone hut hidden amongst the granite – handy in wet weather. Looking to the north north east from here you can see Hare Tor with another mast, your next port of call, ¾ mile away. From the north side of Ger Tor you will see a path heading north north east (21°) towards Hare Tor. Take this, it is clearly marked on the map although is sometimes indistinct underfoot. The descent from Ger Tor is reasonably comfortable walking over tussocky ground and the ascent of Hare Tor, at 531 metres, is not as rough underfoot as the earlier climb up Ger Tor. Once you're on Hare Tor ascend right to the mast as the 360° panoramic view is thirst quenching. Ger Tor looks a mere boy.

From Hare Tor you will see a path heading just slightly south of east (101°). Take this path, which becomes soggy underfoot, to a meeting of small waterways at Deadlake Foot (SX561840). Before you reach Deadlake Foot you will notice the dampness of Dead Lake to your left. At Deadlake Foot there is a stream ahead of you, a combination of Rattle Brook and Green Tor Water which have joined together further north. Turn right here in a southerly direction with the water to your left. Watch your step, it's very wet. When you reach another stream ahead (SX560838) turn right to commence your travels through Tavy Cleave with the River Tavy to your left. This is a stunning area to navigate with its accompanying music of waterfalls – and it's here that we saw ring ouzels. Glance back and around you – it's superb all around. On a warm, sunny day you are also very likely to find basking lizards. This is where the terrain becomes tricky. Please be careful and watch where you put your feet, there is much scrambling. After this

**Tavy Cleave**

Bronze Age hut circles over 3000 years old are evidence of very early settlement in this area and as you stand in this remote spot it's hard to imagine that, more recently, the nearby villages of Mary and Peter Tavy were a thriving mining area. The Reddaford Leat, which features in this walk, was constructed at the beginning of the  19thC. to serve the local mines producing copper, tin, lead, silver – and even arsenic! The Leat runs from Tavy Cleave to Wheal Jewell Reservoir.

The nearest pub, The Elephant's Nest, derives its name from a former, large landlord during the 1950s. As he sat behind the bar serving customers he was described by one of them as looking like an elephant on its nest. The landlord so liked the image that he applied to have the name of the pub changed, although the original name of New Inn still appears on the OS map.

stretch the path becomes clear again and there are inviting places to picnic beside the water, particularly the Devil's Kitchen waterfall (see colour plate). It really is worth the effort of the difficult bit.

Eventually you will see a stone structure on the bank ahead of you. This is where the Mine Leat aqueduct joins the Tavy. Head for this and continue beyond it along the clear path with the leat on your right and the Tavy now away to your left. You are initially heading south west before veering west with the leat. Eventually you see the stone walls of Nattor Farm coming into view on your left. You reach a gate with a bridge over the leat. Continue ahead, soon crossing a stile and still following the leat. About 100 metres further on you will see a little metal 'bridge' which crosses the ditch on your left. Cross it and head towards the farm buildings, picking up a track and bearing right to walk beside the wall on your left. Follow this track back to your car.

*Approaching the magnificent Tavy Cleave*

# Branscombe & the Hooken Undercliff

*This lovely route provides some stunning views, although inevitably this means there are some steepish ascents. It's worth it! The middle section of the walk takes you through the remarkable area of the Hooken Undercliff, a renowned wildlife habitat, and the whole coastline here is part of The Jurassic Coast, England's first Natural World Heritage Site.*

**Map:** OS Explorers: 115, Exmouth & Sidmouth; 116, Lyme Regis & Bridport (both 1:25 000)

**Start point:** Weston (near Sidmouth). Grid ref SY166889

**Distance:** 10 miles / 16km (options for 8 miles / 12.9km and 12 miles / 19.3km)

**Parking:** There are two areas for parking in Weston. One is by the start of the footpath near the ruined Weston House. The other is a charity car park opposite the Acorn Holiday Home Park, where an honesty box is provided for your donation. They are about 200 metres apart

**Refreshments:** The Fountain Head Inn, an ancient, real ale pub in Branscombe: 01297 680359; the Masons Arms, another ancient, real ale pub in Branscombe and although off route in the main part of the village it's worth a visit as the food is very good: 01297 680300; the Old Bakery, a delightful, NT tea rooms and gardens, also in Branscombe: 01752 346585; The Sea Shanty at Branscombe Mouth which does a good range of food: 01297 680577. All the aforementioned should be contacted to confirm opening times as they vary throughout the year. If you reach Beer there is a wide range of pubs, restaurants and beach cafés

**Toilets:** Branscombe Village, near the Village Hall; Branscombe Mouth, in the car park; Beer, near the sea front

**Nearby places to stay:** Bay View Guest House, Beer: 01297 20489; The Masons Arms, Branscombe: 01297 680300; otherwise numerous options in Beer, Branscombe and Sidmouth etc

**Nearby places of interest:** Beer Quarry Caves: 01297 680282; Branscombe Forge: 01752 346585; The Donkey Sanctuary: 01395 578222; Lyme Bay Winery: 01297 551355; Pecorama Model Railway and gardens: 01297 21542; Seaton Tramway: 01297 20375. The Millennium Garden in the centre of Branscombe is open for charity and is worth a visit as you walk past

**Possible birds include:** Buzzard, carrion crow, chiffchaff, cormorant, fulmar, goldfinch, house martin, house sparrow, kestrel, linnet, magpie, raven, swallow, woodpigeon, wren, yellowhammer

**Authors' Tip:** If you don't visit Beer on this walk then pencil it in for another time. We love this village with its beach cafés and the chance to unwind on a seafront, stripy deckchair!

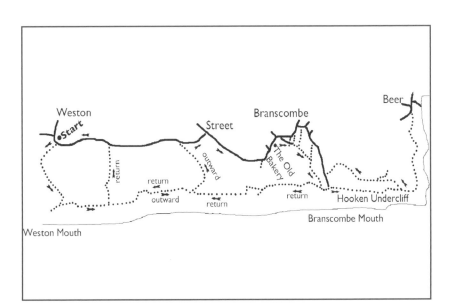

From the non-charity car park a footpath is signed to Weston Mouth and coast path. Take this, passing through the gate and descending on the stony track. This track leads you down through Weston Coombe. Keep on it, ignoring any rights or lefts, as you head down towards the coast. Pass through several gates, until you reach a farm gate and kissing gate with a sign which shows you are entering The National Trust land of Weston Mouth. From here you can see a gate in the top left corner of the field. This is where you need eventually to aim for but the public right of way takes you down to the right to a gate at the bottom, then points you back uphill through the field to this higher gate. Don't descend right down to Weston Mouth unless you want an extremely stiff climb back up.

Once you're at the higher gate pause and look back towards the massive sandstone cliff of High Peak, one of the highest points on the south Devon coast. Once your lungs have recovered continue through the gate, uphill on the hedge-lined path which provides occasional steps to make it slightly easier. The sea is down to your

*Along the Hooken Undercliff*

right. When the path levels out you will be walking quite close to the cliff edge. It's easy walking at this point but please be cautious. The views are fabulous. This is also a good place for butterflies in the summer: marbled white, red admiral and gatekeeper to mention a few possibilities.

When you reach a fingerpost pointing left for Dawes and Weston ignore this and keep ahead, still on the coast path towards Branscombe Mouth, 2.3m. Pass through two more kissing gates and at the second you will see a sign directing you left across the field, slightly in from the coast. This is still the coast path and leads you to a gate in the hedge opposite. Pass through this next gate and turn right, still towards Branscombe Mouth, 2m. Follow the field boundary round to another gate which takes you back onto the headland. Ahead of you is another fingerpost, from here take the left option which directs you to Berry Barton. You are now no longer heading for Branscombe Mouth.

Leave the field through a farm gate, taking the footpath left along a broad, hedged track which can be pretty mucky. This track leads you to a concrete drive at a caravan park and the farm of Berry Barton where you might see peacocks. Keep ahead to the road and turn right, heading down towards Branscombe village. The first area of cottages you reach is Street and home to The Fountain Head Inn. A good stopping place.

From the Inn continue downhill into the main village. This has to be one of the most picturesque places in Devon. Savour it, passing the church on your right, until, ¾ of a mile from the Fountain Head, you reach the Old Bakery on your right, opposite the thatched forge. At this point another refreshment stop is called for and a different kind of savouring.

Walk through the orchard adjacent to the tea gardens, following the path to Manor Mill. This leads through several gates and fields. At the Mill turn left to cross the stream, then 30 metres ahead pick up the footpath signposted right to Branscombe Mouth, ¾m, passing barns on your left. Stay on this path keeping right when it forks and follow it all the way to Branscombe Mouth where it leads you straight to The Sea Shanty – another watering hole.

Those wishing to partake of the shortest of the routes can start to head back at this point, picking up the route from (*) below. But, be advised, if this is your choice you will be missing the most dramatic section of the walk. Those pressing on should cross the river by the car park and take the well-trodden coast path up the hill, signed Beer 2m, aiming for another fingerpost on the hillside ahead of you. Enjoy the views behind you when you pause for breath. At this next fingerpost pass through the gate by the cattle grid, Beer is now 1¾ m, and enter the very attractively situated Sea Shanty Caravan Park. Ahead of you are some spectacular rock stacks along the cliff line which are the haunt of peregrine falcons, the fastest creatures on earth. You have a very good chance of seeing them.

## The Jurassic Coast

The 95 miles of coastline, stretching from Old Harry Rocks at Studland Bay in Dorset to Orcombe Point in East Devon, became England's first UNESCO-selected World Heritage Site in 2001. The geology of the area spans over 180 million years, covering the Triassic, Jurassic and Cretaceous periods. The elegant 'geoneedle' on the coast path at Orcombe Point, Exmouth, the western end of the Jurassic Coast, is a beautiful, modern representation of the rock varieties to be found in the ancient coastline below. Walking the coast path is an excellent way to get a feel for the area but viewing this coastline from the sea is one of the best ways to better understand the history and geology – centuries of erosion have laid history bare. Boat trips are readily available from towns such as Exmouth and Lyme Regis along the coast. The following website gives more information: www.jurassiccoast.com

*Between Branscombe and Weston*

*Looking west towards Branscombe Mouth*

After a short distance through the caravan park a footpath sign will direct you right, Beer is now 1.7m away. This path leads you through a fascinating area of undercliff path with some magnificent cliff formations. More fabulous views await you as you pass between the towering rocks of the Hooken Undercliff. Eventually the path ascends and goes through a kissing gate into the field on top of the cliff. Here another choice awaits you.

For the longest route turn right here and follow the clear path to Beer, 1m further on. This beautiful seaside village is well worth a visit both for its attractive main street and classic stony beach. Should you choose this option you must then retrace your steps back to this gate.

For those returning from this point turn left along the footpath which crosses Hooken Cliffs towards Branscombe Mouth, 1m away. Enjoy more glorious views ahead of you, and look out for fulmars and peregrines in flight below you over the sea. Keep on this path above Hooken Cliffs and East Cliff as it continues westwards to eventually drop down to Branscombe Mouth – it is well signed.

(*) Once back at The Sea Shanty those on the shortest route rejoin from this point. Behind the buildings a kissing gate with a coast path sign points you to Weston Mouth, 2¾m. This is the area of West Cliff. Follow this path with its yellow arrows and acorn way-markers as it leads up to woodland. If you're lucky you may see dolphins in the sea below you. Enter the woodland and keep on up the steps, ignoring any left or right turns. The sea is down to your left and occasional clearings in the woodland afford good views inland to Branscombe village.

Whenever other route options are met continue with the coast path and the acorn signs until you reach a three-way fingerpost.

Although the Fountain Head Inn tempts you straight on, you must turn left here with the coast path for Weston Mouth, 2m. Very soon, at a widening of the path, turn right, once more heading westward along the coast.

Eventually you reach the earlier-encountered fingerpost from whence you walked to Berry Barton. This time keep straight on along the coast path, retracing your steps to the footpath until you reach the kissing gate with a NT sign for Weston Cliff and the footpath leading inland to the right. Take this path for Dawes and Weston.

This clear path leads through a few fields to a tarmac drive. Turn left along it until you reach the road. At which point turn left again to return to Weston and your car.

*Forthcoming CVP titles overleaf*

# Other books published by Culm Valley Publishing

**Title**: *Circular Walks in Central Devon*
**Authors**: Simone Stanbrook-Byrne and James Clancy

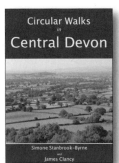

The countryside of central Devon is often overlooked by walkers in favour of the coasts and moors, but it has much to offer: hidden paths, woodlands, patchwork hillsides and deep valleys. Having lived in this area for much of their lives, the authors bring you their collection of favoured routes in out-of-the-way places as well as some better-known Devon beauty spots.
**Walks include**: Culmstock; Huxham; Silverton; Bickleigh; Tiverton; Bolham; Thorverton; Brampford Speke; Kennerleigh; Zeal Monachorum; Shobrooke; Torrington; Withleigh; Rackenford; Butterleigh; Oakford; Stoodleigh; Crediton.

**Publication date**: February 2011
**Pages**: 96pp
**ISBN**: 978-1-907942-01-3
**Format**: Paperback
**Price**: £6.99

---

**Title**: *A Dozen Dramatic Walks in Somerset*
**Authors**: James Clancy and Simone Stanbrook-Byrne

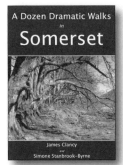

These twelve circular routes, which incorporate some of the county's most stunning scenery, are for walkers who like drama, amazing views and a sense of accomplishment at the end of the day. Taking in some of Somerset's most beautiful landscapes, this book is primarily aimed at those who don't mind putting a little effort into their day's walking. However, options on shorter or easier routes are given where practical for those who prefer less of a challenge.
**Walks include**: Cheddar Gorge; the Exmoor Coast; Dunkery Beacon; Simonsbath; Quantocks; Mendips; etc.

**Publication date**: Spring 2011
**Pages**: 88pp
**ISBN**: 978-1-907942-02-0
**Format**: Paperback
**Price**: £5.99

---

**Title**: *A Dozen Dramatic Walks in Cornwall*
**Authors**: James Clancy and Simone Stanbrook-Byrne

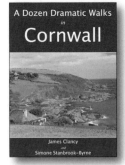

The drama and beauty encountered in Devon and Somerset is now continued further west in Cornwall with no lessening of the quality of walking.
In keeping with other titles in the series, each route includes details of local watering holes for refreshment, places to stay and nearby places of interest. Historic notes, authors' tips and pointers on natural history are also included.
**Walks include**: Bodmin Moor; Tintagel; Lamorna Cove; Helford Estuary; Talland Bay/Polperro; etc.

**Publication date**: September 2011
**Pages**: 88pp
**ISBN**: 978-1-907942-03-7
**Format**: Paperback
**Price**: £5.99

Orders can be placed at www.culmvalleypublishing.co.uk
or alternatively by telephone on 01884 849085